Debt-Free Living
A Journey to Financial Empowerment

Table of Contents

Chapter 1. Introduction

Immerse yourself in an empowering journey towards financial freedom in our Special Report on "Debt-Free Living: A Journey to Financial Empowerment". Escape from the oppressive chains of debt and revitalise your life with safe, proven strategies that will not only help you eliminate your debt but keep it off for good! With an approachable and cheerful style, this report simplifies the complex world of personal finance, giving you the tools you need to reclaim your life from debt's clutches. It's more than just a report; it's your personal guide to a future filled with possibilities, confidence, and importantly, peace of mind. Take control of your financial destiny - it all begins with a single step and this special report is the ideal place to start!

Chapter 2. Understanding the Debt Trap: Roots and Consequences

The enchanting allure of modern consumerism has led many of us to embrace the familiar yet destructive habit of living beyond our means. The relentless pursuit of immediate gratification often blinds us to the long-term effects of accumulating debt. This phenomenon, referred to as the 'debt trap', is a critical factor hindering our financial empowerment and freedom.

2.1. The Origination of Debt

In order to fully understand the depth and influence of the debt trap, it is crucial to trace its origins. The concept of debt–borrowing from another with the intention of repayment–is not new. In fact, it dates back to the earliest recorded human civilizations, where borrowing and lending took place in the form of goods and services. However, the nature of debt has drastically transformed over time.

The paradigm shift occurred with the advent of credit cards and consumer lending programs. These are well-thought out, strategic tools introduced by financial institutions to aid consumers in their purchasing power. While their existence isn't inherently toxic, the misuse of these credit instruments can lead us into a revolving cycle of debt.

2.2. How We Fall into the Debt Trap

Falling into the debt trap seems effortless, almost natural, especially when we're enticed by the commodified notion of the 'good life'. The cycle usually begins innocently, perhaps with the purchase of an expensive gadget on credit. The item, though non-essential, becomes an emotional want that supersedes sensible judgment. When the first few bills arrive, they may be manageable. However, over time, as we lean more on credit, the unpaid balances rise, leading to an increase in monthly repayments.

Next, we arrive at a stage known as 'Minimum Payment Syndrome'. At this point, instead of focusing on our total outstanding balance, we happily content ourselves by paying just the minimum balance required each month. It is here that most of us lose sight of our increasing debt, as we continue fueling our habits of unchecked consumption.

2.3. The Consequences of the Debt Trap

Uncontrolled debt significantly impacts various aspects of our life. Firstly, we face the incessant stress of coping with mounting bills, which can render our financial situation desperate. Studies have shown a direct link between unpaid debt and mental health issues such as anxiety and depression.

Furthermore, debt often leads to strained relationships, as financial instability inadvertently affects our interactions with family and friends. The ripple effect of the debt trap is prevalent in societal levels too, with debt-related issues contributing to homelessness, bankruptcy, and arguably, economic recession.

Also, a low credit score, one of the sleights of hand of the debt trap, impacts our borrowing capacity and access to vital resources. Consequently, we fall further into the trap, turning to alternatives like payday loans, which perpetuate the vicious cycle of borrowing and owing.

2.4. Escaping the Debt Trap

Escaping the debt trap requires not only a clear understanding of the vicious cycle of debt but also determination and discipline to follow through with practical steps towards a healthier financial lifestyle. This involves reducing unnecessary spending, creating and strictly adhering to an effective budget, including an emergency fund, focusing on paying off high-interest debt first, and seeking professional help when necessary.

The process of freeing ourselves from the shackles of debt isn't immediate, and pitfalls are inevitable during this journey. However, the ultimate reward of financial independence outweighs the temporary sacrifices made.

Remember, our economic behavior impacts not just our individual financial health, but also contributes to the overall wellbeing of our community. By recognizing the roots and consequences of our financial choices, we can begin to break the chain of habitual borrowing, thus positioning ourselves for a life that allows us to experience true financial freedom.

Chapter 3. Changing Mindsets: Building a Positive Attitude Towards Saving

The very first step on your journey to financial freedom is to cultivate an attitude poised towards saving. This is fundamental and can be inculcated regardless of your current financial circumstances. So let's dive into how you can foster this crucial mindset.

3.1. The Power of Mindset

Remember, the mind is a powerful tool, and your financial destiny is directly shaped by your mindset about money and budgeting. If you adopt a positive mindset towards saving, it reflects in your attitudes, habits, decisions, and interactions with money.

Our mindsets are generally influenced by previous experiences, upbringing, and societal perspectives. Therefore, shifting to a positive attitude towards saving may require conscious, often challenging, behaviour adjustments. However, the outcome will be rewarding.

3.2. Unearthing Your Current Financial Mindset

Understanding your current financial mindset is crucial to determine where you need to focus your effort to change. To do this, you need to introspect. Have an honest conversation with yourself. Ask questions such as:

- How do you feel about money?

- How do you view saving?

- Are you comfortable discussing money?

- What are your short-, medium-, and long-term financial goals?

- What are your spending habits?

Understanding your answers will provide you a clear snapshot of your current money mindset and pathway to inculcate saving-oriented behaviours.

3.3. The Shift to a Saving Mindset

Turning your mindset around for the better involves formulating a conscious action plan. Change doesn't come automatically. It requires time, patience, and consistent practice. Here's a roadmap to make that shift easier.

1. Establish clear financial goals.

2. Allocate a purpose for every dollar you earn.

3. Practice restraint in spending.

4. Make saving a priority.

3.4. Establish Clear Financial Goals

Clear, achievable financial goals act as a guide map leading you to your ultimate financial destination, giving your saving efforts direction and purpose. Whether it's home ownership, creating an emergency fund, retirement, or even a dream vacation, a clear vision of these planned financial objectives will motivate and push you towards a strong saving culture.

3.5. Allocate a Purpose for Every Dollar

Consider adopting a zero-based budget, where you assign every dollar you earn a job. Instead of viewing your income as disposable, see it as a tool to help you reach your financial targets.

For example, if you earn 1000 dollars, determine how it can be divided across bills, savings, investments, and more. Doing so will not only give you fiscal discipline but also implicate you to perceive savings as an integral part of your financial partitioning.

3.6. Practice Restraint in Spending

The desire to make impulsive purchases can be intense. However, learning to resist these temptations is paramount for savings growth. Develop a better understanding of your needs versus your wants.

Before making a purchase decision, take a moment to analyse your motivation. If it's not something you genuinely need, consider skipping it and putting that money towards your savings instead.

3.7. Make Saving a Priority

Generally, we tend to save what is left after spending. However, that strategy will rarely yield a robust savings account. Aim to save first and then spend what is left. Saving must be given as much importance as paying utility bills and other necessary outlays. This subtle shift in approach can become your financial game changer.

3.8. Incorporating Positivity and Patience

Changing your financial mindset isn't a one-time event. It's a journey. There will be periods of setbacks and even failures. However, maintaining an optimistic attitude and staying patient through these phases is crucial. Every setback is a lesson, and every lesson brings you one step closer to your goal.

The path to cultivating a positive attitude towards saving isn't always straightforward. It involves breaking down barriers and overcoming deeply ingrained behaviours. It requires commitment, patience, and resilience. Yet, once this journey is set in motion and embraced fully, the transformation is profound. Your financial goals seem achievable, your debts manageable, and a debt-free life, a tangible reality. Most importantly, you start cherishing the peace of mind that comes with financial empowerment.

Remember, it all begins with a change in mindset. It's your first step towards reclaiming control over your life from the clutches of debt and stepping into a future filled with security and financial freedom.

Chapter 4. The Power of Budgeting: Guiding Your Spending Wisely

It can be said with a fair amount of certainty that the key to unlocking the doors of financial freedom lies in developing a sound budgetary plan. A budget works as a financial blueprint, exhibiting where your money comes from, how much of it there is, and finally, where it all goes. Let's take a closer look at how budgeting can play a crucial role in helping you guide your spending wisely.

4.1. Budgeting Basics

Just as an architect relies on a blueprint to guide a building's construction, a budget will serve as a financial blueprint for you. The first task in creating a budget is determining your income. Accumulate all sources of money flowing your way, including salary, interest, dividends and any other sources of income you may have.

Once your income is determined, the next stage is recognizing your expenses. Split them into two categories: fixed and discretionary. Fixed expenses are those that remain relatively or absolutely same over a period of time, like rent or mortgage payments, utility bills, and car payments. Discretionary expenditures, on the other hand, are variable costs such as groceries, entertainment, and dining out.

At this point, you've outlined the skeleton of your budget. The next step is doing the math... simply subtract your expenses from your income.

4.2. The Magic of Compromise

One of the key sides of budgeting that often goes unconsidered is compromise. It's crucial to understand that budgeting often means making tough decisions about what expenses to reduce or possibly eliminate. Be prepared to distinguish between wants and needs, and prioritize needs over wants, always.

It's also essential to acknowledge and tackle "hidden" expenses that might not be immediately evident. These could include those daily cups of coffee, those non-essential wardrobe updates, weekly outings, and more. Cutting down on these incidental costs can end up saving you a considerable amount over time.

4.3. The Power of Prioritization

When operating within a budget, you often have to make choices. Prioritization will be your guiding force. Start by shortlisting and ranking your expenses according to importance.

Make sure you're meeting crucial expenses such as housing, food, and healthcare. After these essentials are taken care of, funds should go towards other necessary but less immediate costs, like clothing or transportation. Finally, discretionary expenses like entertainment or eating out are the last to be taken into account.

4.4. Commitment: The Backbone of Success

Assiduously keeping a budget is not a one-time activity; it's a long-term commitment. It's important to review and reassess your budget regularly and adjust according to changes in income or expenses.

Again, remember that budgeting is about making compromises and sacrifices to meet financial goals. It's perfectly fine to have entertainment and indulgence expenses, but they should be planned and reasonable. Temptation exists, but with determination, even those urges to splurge could be controlled.

4.5. Making Saving a Habit

One of the most powerful habits to adapt from budgeting is saving. Incorporating savings into your budget propels you towards financial empowerment faster than you may think. Habitually putting aside a particular portion of your income as savings is key. Remember, a part of what you earn is yours to keep!

This saving could be used to build an emergency fund, saving for down payment for a home, children's education, or even filling up your retirement coffers. With a well-devised budget and a savings habit, you would be truly driving your finances, rather than letting them drive you.

4.6. The Role of Tools and Resources

In these high-tech times, numerous tools can aid in budgeting and tracking expenses. Smartphone applications, online tools, and software like Mint, YNAB (You Need a Budget), and Quicken can save time and offer in-depth insight into your budget and spending habits. Don't shy away from leaning on into these tools to make your budgeting task simpler and more effective.

In conclusion, mastering the art of budgeting is a journey. Remember that it's not just about managing money, but an endeavour towards your bigger life goals, wealth aspirations, and ultimely, financial freedom. Embrace budgeting as a way of life, managing your finances wisely, and watch as the power of budgeting transforms your journey towards financial empowerment!

Chapter 5. Defeating Debt: Step-by-Step Strategies toward Debt Freedom

Understanding Your Debt Situation === Getting to Know the Enemy

The first step in defeating debt is understanding what you're up against. A thorough examination of your financial status is critical. Start by listing all your debts. Include credit card balances, personal loans, student loans, mortgages, auto loans, and any money you owe to friends or family. For each debt, note the total amount, interest rate, and minimum monthly payment.

Using this information, determine the total amount of debt you have and the total amount you pay every month. This complete view of your financial health will help you develop a strategy to become debt-free.

5.1. Measuring Your Debt-to-Income Ratio

A vital tool in understanding your financial health is the debt-to-income ratio. This ratio shows the percentage of your monthly gross income that goes towards paying debts.

To calculate this ratio:

1. Add up all your monthly debt payments.

2. Determine your gross monthly income before taxes.

3. Divide the monthly payments by the gross income.

4. Multiply the result by 100 to get a percentile.

Let's say your monthly debt commitments are $2000, and your monthly gross income is $5000. Your debt-to-income ratio will then be 40%. A ratio over 40% can cause alarm bells to ring for lenders.

Creating a Game Plan === Developing a Budget

Regardless of the size of your debt, a well-thought-out budget can help you regain control. Begin by mapping out your income and expenses. Once you have a clear overview, look for areas where you can cut costs.

Consider using a budget tracking app or software to help you identify spending patterns and areas for improvement. Remember, the intention here is not to cause distress but rather to make smarter financial choices.

5.2. Prioritizing Debts

Not all debts are created equal. Some, like mortgages and student loans, are considered "good" debts because they leverage long-term benefits or have lower interest rates.

On the other hand, "bad" debts, like credit card debt and payday loans, have high interest rates and do not provide any return on the money borrowed.

It's usually best to prioritize the repayment of bad debts first. This process, known as debt avalanche, focuses on paying off the highest-interest-rates debts first and moving to the next.

Implementing Debt Eradication Strategies === Using the Staff of Discipline: The Debt Avalanche

As mentioned, the debt avalanche method prioritizes debts with the highest interest rate. It involves making the minimum payments on all debts and then using any leftover money to pay off the debt with the highest interest rate. This approach saves money and time but requires discipline, as constantly paying off high-interest debt can feel like a never-ending battle.

5.3. The Shield of Momentum: The Debt Snowball

The debt snowball method, on the other hand, targets debts with the smallest balance first. This strategy creates a sense of achievement and momentum but could result in paying more overall if high-interest debts are not paid off quickly.

Decide which strategy works best for your situation and stick to it.

5.4. Embracing the Power of Debt Consolidation

Debt consolidation can be a useful strategy for those struggling with multiple debts. It involves combining all debts into one with lower interest rates or more manageable monthly payments. It simplifies the process and makes debt management easier.

Boosting Your Pay Downs === Using Windfalls Wisely

Bonuses, tax refunds, inheritances, or any unexpected income are windfall opportunities. Instead of spending these on non-essential items, consider using them to make extra payments towards your debt. It can significantly accelerate your debt payoff plan.

5.5. Side Hustling for Extra Cash

Consider starting a side hustle to generate additional income. It could be anything from freelance work, to selling handcrafted items online, to house sitting. The revenue you make from these can provide a huge boost to your debt reduction efforts.

Staying Debt-Free === Building an Emergency Fund

Having an emergency fund is like owning a financial safety net. It safeguards you against the unexpected, preventing you from slipping back into debt. Aim to save a fund that can cover 3 to 6 months' worth of living expenses.

5.6. Creating and Adapting a New Lifestyle

Finally, living debt-free involves changing your lifestyle and developing a healthier relationship with money. Living within your means, using credit responsibly, and continuously saving and investing for the future should become your new norm.

Defeating debt and achieving financial freedom seems like an elusive dream for many, but with dedication, discipline, and well-planned strategies, this dream can become a reality. Remember, the journey to debt-free living is just that - a journey. Be steadfast, compassionate with yourself and maintain your momentum until you cross the finish line. You've got this!

Chapter 6. Alternatives to Borrowing: Less Common Ways to Fund Big Purchases

Before diving into the myriad of alternatives to borrowing, it is crucial to understand why it is necessary to search for these alternatives in the first place. When we think about making large purchases, typically homes, cars, or a college education, it is almost second nature to consider loans or borrowing as the primary method to finance these big-ticket items. The reason being, it's the norm handed down to us by generations and reinforced by culture and financial institutions.

However, reliance on loans or borrowing money to finance big purchases often leads to a cycle of debt. These debts become chains that gradually erode your financial freedom and stability, putting stress on your life. Exploring alternatives to borrowing can empower you to make significant purchases in a fiscally responsible way, minus the crushing weight of debt.

6.1. Saving vs. Borrowing

The first place to start when looking at alternatives to borrowing is adopting a saving culture. The power of saving money over time cannot be overstated. Money saved, not borrowed, is what empowers you - giving you freedom to make choices, enabling you to handle emergencies without sinking into panic-or-debt mode, and assisting you in preparing for the future.

Here are some steps to cultivate a saving habit:

- Prioritize Savings: Think of savings as mandatory spending, just like your bills. Pay yourself first before other bills and expenses.

Consider automating your savings if you find it challenging to save manually.

- Set Achievable Goals: Take time to determine your short, medium, and long term financial goals. These goals will serve as a motivation to maintain the discipline to save.

- Create a Budget: A budget is an essential tool that helps you direct where your money should go. Regular review of your budget aids in adjusting your saving and spending habits.

6.2. Crowdfunding

In recent years, crowdfunding has emerged as a unique, community-driven way to raise funds, particularly for projects or causes. Platforms like Kickstarter, GoFundMe and Indiegogo provide a space for people to share their financial needs with a broad audience.

Individuals seeking to finance large projects can set up a campaign, often offering rewards to those who donate certain amounts. Though typically associated with technological innovations or artistic ventures, crowdfunding can be an alternative for major personal expenses if you can provide a compelling story or cause.

While there are the usual internet scams to be wary of, careful selection of your platform and thorough research should help mitigate the risks.

6.3. Rent-to-Own Options

Rent-to-own schemes allow you to rent an item for a set period, at the end of which, you have the option to buy it.

This option is most common for household items like appliances or furniture, but can also be used for larger purchases like houses or cars. It is a good alternative for individuals who do not immediately have the resources to make a significant purchase but will have it over time.

However, it comes with a caveat: these schemes are typically more expensive than an outright purchase. Also, if you decide not to buy the item, the money spent on rent is not refunded. This option should weigh well against other alternatives before venturing into it.

6.4. Trading Services or Bartering

Trading services or bartering can work as an excellent alternative to borrowing, especially when you have a particular skill-set that others find valuable. These trades typically don't involve money and allow you to acquire something you need by exchanging a service you can provide. A plumber, for instance, can fix a mechanic's sink in return for car repairs.

The downside to this approach is that it requires a certain level of negotiation and the ability to find matching wants and needs, making it less straightforward than simply buying an item with money.

6.5. Saving Bonds and Certificates

Savings Bonds are government-issued securities designed for long-term investments that pay interest after a fixed period, frequently used to finance large purchases. They are considered very safe and ideal for risk-averse investors.

Similarly, certificates of deposit (CDs) let you invest your money for a specified length of time, and, in return, the bank guarantees you a specific interest rate. Because you agree to leave your money for a set period, these often have higher interest rates than standard savings accounts. However, there may be penalties for withdrawing your money before the time expires.

As you can see, there are many alternatives to borrowing when planning to finance significant purchases. These range from the more common like saving, to the unconventional like crowdfunding and bartering. Understanding the pros and cons of each can help you make informed decisions that suit your financial situation and minimize your dependence on loans and borrowing, leading you to a more empowered financial future.

Chapter 7. Emergency Funds: Your Safety Net Against Debt

Among the first steps towards financial strength and independence is having readily accessible funds set aside for emergencies. Known as an emergency fund, this portion of savings serves as a safety net against potential pitfalls along the journey to debt-free living. Keeping finances in order is about more than just having money in the bank; it's about having control over financial stability, particularly during unexpected occurrences.

7.1. Understanding the Role of an Emergency Fund

An emergency fund is a cash reserve that you set aside to cover unexpected expenses. Its role is to offer a financial buffer which can cover expenses like repairs, medical bills, sudden loss of income, or other financial surprises. Most importantly, an emergency fund prevents one from sinking into debt when these unexpected hurdles arise.

Financial gurus typically recommend having three to six months worth of expenses set aside. The justification behind this advice is to provide coverage in case of a sudden job loss, where half a year's worth of buffer buys you valuable time for job hunting without falling into debt. However, for individuals or families with inconsistent income, more savings may be advisable.

7.2. Building Your Emergency Fund

Getting started on an emergency fund can seem daunting – especially when juggling other financial goals. The key is to make regular, incremental savings that will build up to three, six months, or more worth of living expenses.

1. Begin by setting a goal: Refer to your budget and calculate your monthly expenses. Multiply this by 3 or 6 to get the target for your emergency fund.

2. Open a separate savings account for your fund: As the purpose of an emergency fund is to be readily accessible when needed, an accessible savings account that does not penalize for withdrawals or transfers is essential.

3. Automate your savings: Set automatic monthly transfers from your checking account to your emergency fund to ensure consistency.

4. Cut down on non-essential expenses: Temporarily reduce spending on non-essential items like dining out, entertainment, and vacations. Reallocate these savings towards your emergency fund.

5. Generate additional income: Consider turning your hobbies into a side business to generate additional income that can supplement your emergency savings.

7.3. Nurturing Your Fund

Once your fund is set, the journey isn't over. It's essential to nurture its growth, regularly evaluate its adequacy, and replenish withdrawals.

1. Review your budget annually: As expenses evolve over time due to factors like inflation, changes in lifestyle and family situations, it's crucial to review your budget and adjust your emergency fund target accordingly.

2. Replenish used funds: If you dip into your fund for an emergency, make sure to replenish it as soon as you can, maintaining its

ability to cover your expenses for the determined number of months.

3. Prioritize your emergency fund: Your fund should be a financial priority, so be deliberate about nurturing its growth. Resist the temptation to skip contributions or use the money for non-emergency situations.

7.4. Making Use of Your Emergency Fund

Your emergency fund is there for you when you need it, but what constitutes an emergency? Necessary expenses qualify as emergencies, e.g., car repair, medical bills, sudden unemployment, urgent home repairs, etc. When these situations arise, do not hesitate to use your fund; that's precisely what it's there for!

7.5. The Impact of an Emergency Fund on Debt Management

Having an emergency fund lowers your risk of incurring high-interest debt in times of financial troubles. Rather than relying on credit cards, loans, or other forms of debt, your emergency fund provides the buffer needed without further damaging your financial health. And importantly, it provides you with peace of mind, knowing you have a financial safety net.

In conclusion, an emergency fund is a solid foundation on your journey towards financial empowerment. With it, not only will you be able to handle unexpected expenses, but you will also avoid falling back into the trap of debt. Careful planning, dedicated saving, and judicious use of your emergency fund can lead to a confident and liberating debt-free living. Remember, it all starts with one step, and the first step is understanding the importance of, and building, your emergency fund.

Chapter 8. Credit Cards: Taming the Plastic Beast

The glittering sheen of a credit card can be beguiling. An asset that allows you to buy now and pay later - what's not to love, right? However, before long, this charming plastic can turn into a monstrous beast if not used responsibly. In the fight against debt, your credit card can either be your strongest ally or your fiercest adversary. But worry not, dear reader, because taming this plastic beast is an attainable feat.

8.1. Understanding Credit Cards MoA

To effectively wield the power of credit cards without succumbing to the crushing burden of debt, understanding their modus operandi is crucial.

Credit cards are essentially a revolving line of credit provided by financial institutions. When you make a purchase using a credit card, you are essentially borrowing money from the card issuer. This borrowed sum has to be paid back within a predetermined period, known as the grace period. If you manage to clear the balance within this grace period, you usually will not be charged any interest. If not, the unpaid balance will be carried over to the next billing cycle, and the card issuer can charge you interest on the outstanding balance. This is where the debt spiral begins.

8.2. Interest and the Concept of Annual Percentage Rate

If we were to nominate the most potent weapon in the credit card beast's arsenal, it would undoubtedly be the interest rate, more specifically, the Annual Percentage Rate (APR). Simply put, APR is the cost of borrowing on a yearly basis. It's calculated as a yearly rate and can range from approximately 18% to over 25% depending on your creditworthiness and the card issuer's policies.

To illustrate the APR concept, suppose you have an outstanding balance of $1,000 on your credit card at the end of the billing cycle, and your card has an APR of 24%.2. If this balance remains unpaid for a year, you would owe the card issuer an additional $240 (24% of $1,000) at year-end. Imagine the debt size if the outstanding balance goes unchecked for a few months, or even years.

8.3. The Minimum Payment Trap

Another tricky aspect is the concept of the minimum payment. Each month, your credit card statement will display two figures: your total outstanding balance and your minimum monthly payment. Simply, the minimum payment is the smallest amount you can pay on your credit card bill to keep your account in good standing, typically a small percentage (2-3%) of the total balance.

Although meeting the minimum payment seems attractive, especially when tight on money, it's a trap. Only making minimum payments can lead to interest charges rapidly accumulating on the remaining balance. Over time, this leads to much higher overall repayment. So, while it might keep your account current, minimum payments contribute heavily to the growth of debt - making it a crucial part to understand and avoid on the journey to debt-free living.

8.4. Wisely Utilizing Credit Card Rewards

But it's not all doom and gloom. Credit cards can play an effective role in managing your finances if used wisely. One key feature is credit card rewards. Many card issuers offer various incentives to encourage spending on their cards, like cash backs, air miles, or points that can be exchanged for goods and services.

If used properly, these reward schemes can help you make substantial savings. However, they are often a double-edged sword. The temptation of rewards can lead to overspending and, eventually, falling into debt. Remember, the reward is not a justification to spend beyond your capability. To really reap the benefits, always pay off your card balance in full every month.

8.5. Making Credit Cards a Tool, Not a Liability

The secret to financial empowerment lies in making your credit card a tool rather than a liability. Some simple, yet essential, steps and strategies to adopt include:

- Pay your card balance in full, on time, every month.

- Understand all terms, fees, and penalties associated with your card.

- Leverage rewards wisely and avoid overspending to gain rewards.

- Regularly review your credit card statements to monitor spending and identify any fraudulent activities.

- Employ your credit card for budgeting: Use it for monthly expenses and clear the balance immediately - a disciplined approach that helps track outgoings and control spendings.

Credit cards could either lead to a debt trap or become a useful financial tool: the outcome entirely depends on you. Tackling the credit card beast may seem like a daunting task initially but, with understanding, disciplined application, you can surely tame it and shift the scales towards financial empowerment. Remember: you are not alone in this journey and this guide is here to walk alongside you, illuminating your path every step of the way.

Chapter 9. Living Below Your Means: A Viable Path to Debt-Free

When it comes to keeping debt at bay, one of the most viable strategies to explore is living below your means. This is not just about reducing unwanted expenses, but a whole new approach to how you earn, spend and save money. Now, let's delve deeper into this subject and give you a detailed understanding of how you can incorporate this golden rule of personal finance into your life.

9.1. Recognising the Difference between Wants and Needs

To begin your journey towards living below your means, the primary step is differentiating between your needs and your wants. A 'need' is something you must have for survival, such as food, shelter, or medical care, while a 'want' is something you would like to have, but can live without.

Needs	Wants
Food and Water	Dining at High-End Restaurants
Basic Clothing	Designer Fashion
Shelter	Luxury Condo
Basic Utilities	Expensive Electronics
Essential medication and medical services	Luxuries like massage and spa treatments

Remember, just because you want something doesn't mean you need it. Needs should always be prioritised over wants, as this can significantly reduce your expenses and increase your saving potential.

9.2. Minimising Expenses

Once you've sorted out your needs and wants, the next step is to curtail unnecessary expenses. Here are some areas where you may be able to save:

- Cable TV: Switch to lower-priced platforms like Netflix or Amazon Prime for entertainment.

- Insurance: Choose insurance policies that adequately cover your needs without costing a fortune.

- Groceries: Plan your meals ahead and buy bulk to save on food costs.

- Utilities: Use energy-efficient appliances to reduce utility bills.

- Recreation: Find low-cost or free activities for entertainment.

Evaluate every expense category in your budget and explore ways to reduce costs without significantly impacting your lifestyle.

9.3. Optimising Income

Living below your means isn't just about spending less. It's also about making more. Job stability might not always be in your hands, so having additional income streams can offer more control over your finances.

- Freelancing or part-time work can supplement your regular income.

- Investing in the stock market or real estate can generate strong returns over the long run.

- Starting a small home-based business can bring in extra income.

- Hone your skills and seek promotion or better job opportunities.

Don't limit your financial growth to just your monthly salary. Explore opportunities and diversify your income streams.

9.4. Savings and Investment

Saving is the cornerstone of financial health.

- Contribute a certain amount or percentage of your income to savings regularly.
- Consider higher-yield savings accounts or certificates of deposit.
- Build an emergency fund to cover 3-6 months worth of living expenses.
- Invest in retirement funds.

Investing is another path to ensuring long-term financial security.

- Mutual funds and bonds are typically less risky, offering consistent modest returns.
- Equity or real estate may give higher returns, albeit with greater risk.
- Diversify your investment portfolio to spread the risk.

9.5. Saying No to Debt

Avoiding debt is an integral part of living below your means.

- Use credit cards responsibly, and pay the full balance each month.
- Avoid high-interest or bad loans.
- Pay debts on time to avoid penalties and maintain your credit score.

- For necessary loans (mortgage or car), ensure your income supports these additional debt repayments.

In summary, living below your means can be an effective strategy to evade the chains of debt, ensuring you're never living paycheck to paycheck and always have financial security to fall back on. It doesn't require a lifestyle of extreme frugality. Instead, it's a balanced approach to income, spending, and saving that allows for a comfortable and secure life, free of financial stress. It might take some time to make these changes and see results, but as with any journey, the important thing is to start. After all, financial freedom and empowerment are just around the corner.

Chapter 10. Avoiding Debt Relapse: Maintaining Your Financial Health

You've worked hard, made sacrifices, and followed a planned approach to becoming debt-free. Congratulations on achieving this crucial financial milestone! Now, the challenge lies in maintaining this state of financial health, also known as avoiding debt relapse.

10.1. The essence of avoiding debt relapse

Akin to an individual who has overcome any form of addiction, you must learn to avoid temptation and stay on the right path. Financial health is an ongoing commitment that necessitates deliberate actions and consistent discipline. Equally important is understanding the sources of financial trouble that could push you back into debt.

To begin this journey, it is essential to understand your relationship with money and how it influences your behaviour. It would be best if you thrived on making conscious and informed financial decisions, rather than being swayed by your emotions or temporary impulses. Remember, financial empowerment comes from taking charge of your finance, not letting them control you.

10.2. Building a reliable and robust financial plan

To maintain financial health, having a comprehensive financial plan in place is crucial. It serves as your roadmap to financial stability. Your plan should include a monthly budget where you track your income and expenses, investments for long-term goals, an emergency savings fund, and regular assessments of your financial status.

A budget is a foundational element in avoiding debt relapse. Setting and adhering to a realistic budget that accounts for all your income and expenses helps constrain your spending and eliminate unnecessary expenditures. Applications and tools are available that can aid you in tracking your income and expenses and ensuring your budget's adherence.

Creating an emergency savings fund is another critical strategy in your financial plan. An emergency fund is your financial safety net during unexpected circumstances, such as a sudden job loss or unexpected medical bills. Experts generally recommend having three to six months of living expenses set aside in such a fund.

In addition to an emergency fund, investments play an essential role in building wealth and maintaining financial health. Investments not only provide income for your retirement but also help you reach significant long-term financial goals such as buying a house or funding your children's higher education.

Lastly, a regular evaluation of your financial health is essential. Regular check-ins, preferably quarterly or biannually, will help you assess your financial status, help identify areas for improvement, and ensure you're on track with your financial goals.

10.3. Revisiting and redefining your lifestyle

Redefining your lifestyle is a vital part of avoiding debt relapse. This does not mean giving up on all your desires or living in austerity. Instead, it is about living within your means, valuing experiences or intrinsic aspects more than material possessions and prioritizing needs over wants.

It would help if you practiced deliberate spending, asking yourself whether a purchase is genuinely necessary or is influenced by your desires. By prioritizing needs over wants, you can reduce non-essential spending, increase your savings, and thereby further solidify your journey towards financial health.

In addition, you should aim to nurture a habit of saving. Consider it as paying yourself first. Experts often suggest saving at least 20% of your income. However, you can start with a lower percentage, gradually increasing it over time.

10.4. Building financial literacy

Finally, building financial literacy is critical to staying out of debt and remaining financially healthy. Financial literacy is your understanding of how money works, including managing personal finances, investing, and understanding and using financial products effectively.

Being financially literate will empower you to make informed financial decisions, reducing your chances of falling into debt. This includes understanding the use and potential dangers of credit cards, knowing how to calculate interest rates, being aware of tax implications, and more. There are numerous free and paid resources available, from books and podcasts to online courses and seminars, local community education programs, or speaking to a financial adviser, where you can improve your financial literacy skills.

In conclusion, avoiding debt relapse and maintaining financial health is as much about psychological well-being as it is about financial stability. Retaining and increasing awareness about the factors affecting your financial health, creating a strong financial plan, redefining your lifestyle, and building your financial literacy can help you prevent a debt relapse. Remember, financial empowerment is a continuous journey, and every step you take towards it brings you closer to a future filled with possibilities!

Chapter 11. Celebrating Financial Empowerment: Life Beyond Debt

Few experiences are as liberating as discharging the last of your debts and setting your ambitions free. The moment when you've paid every cent is transformative; it's when economic freedom becomes a reality, not an aspiration. Aside from the practicalities, life beyond debt is a journey of moments just waiting to be celebrated.

11.1. The Journey to Freedom: The Last Payment

The last payment is a triumphant day, reminiscent of conquering Everest's peak. It's a milestone that demands recognition, encapsulating years of dedication and sacrifice. By celebrating, you not only honor your achievement but also set a precedent for your new path. Positive reinforcement is crucial in maintaining our new financial behaviors, and there's no better reinforcement than a hearty cheer for success.

Some choose to ring in their victory with grand affairs, while others prefer intimate recognition. Both serve to acknowledge the effort, resilience, and commitment required to navigate debt's tyranny.

11.2. Relishing in Financial Stability

Whilst the celebration of the last payment is a single event, you can also find joy in the quieter, everyday experiences that financial stability brings, like the comfort of a paid-off home, the security of a sturdy emergency fund, or the freedom to spend without guilt. This is the point where discipline, patience, and perseverance converge.

11.3. Cultivating a Positive Money Mindset

The journey doesn't end here. You must cultivate a positive money mindset, essential in maintaining financial empowerment. Remember, your experiences with debt have educated you, not defined you. Embrace the wisdom garnered from your journey and use it to shape a healthier financial future. This involves iterative learning from past spending habits, understanding your influencing attitudes towards money, and nurturing a healthy relationship with it.

11.4. Navigating Your Days Debt-Free

Living debt-free is both exhilarating and daunting. It gives you the autonomy to make financial decisions without the constant worry of loans on your shoulder. The power to save, invest, and spend according to your needs is at your fingertips.

At the same time, the newfound freedom can be overwhelming. The key is to stay committed to your financial plan and not fall back into old habits. You must maintain a steadfast financial discipline; this is your armor against future financial turmoil, preventing your descent back into debt. Regular governance of your expenses, wise spending, and disciplined saving are vital habits to acquire.

11.5. Expanding Financial Horizons: Investing and Growing Wealth

With the eradication of debt, your ability to build wealth increases significantly. This chapter of your journey should focus on investments and wealth growth. Whether it's real estate, stocks, bonds, or a retirement plan, intelligent investing contributes to financial stability in the long term. It's the strategic move from mere survival to thriving, reinforcing your financial empowerment to new heights.

11.6. Giving Back: The Spirit of Sharing

Financial empowerment also instigates the spirit of giving back. With the newfound stability, you have the capacity to support causes you believe in and make a difference. Whether it's sponsoring a child's education, donating to a charity, or supporting a local community event, using your financial empowerment to uplift others is a testament to freedom from debt. It's a powerful way of celebrating your journey and using your freedom to contribute to society constructively.

11.7. Embracing Your Debt-Free Future

With the burden of debt released, you are free to design your financial future. This could involve plans for early retirement, traveling the world, or launching a dream business. Whatever the dream, life beyond debt enables you to pursue it without fear.

11.8. Building a Legacy

Obtaining financial empowerment isn't solely about you. It's also a powerful legacy to pass on. Encouraging and practicing financial empowerment in your community, your household, and particularly with your children, gifts them with a reach that extends beyond monetary value; it equips them with the tools to build strong, independent lives less susceptible to financial hardship.

In conclusion, the journey of life beyond debt is a validation of your resilience, proof of your power over your financial destiny, and testament to a future filled with possibilities. Celebrate it, cherish it, and most importantly, utilize this power for self-growth and community development. Your journey from debt to financial empowerment is more than just an economical transition; it is an elevation towards an enriched life and a secure future.